HOW TO CLEAN WINDOWS LIKE THE PROS

HOW TO CLEAN WINDOWS LIKE THE PROS

**THE FIRST COMPLETE BOOK ON HOW TO
CLEAN WINDOWS THE PROFESSIONAL WAY**

Written By
John Baxter

Illustrated by
Jim Dilts

DISCLAIMER NOTICE

This book is not intended to be a comprehensive instruction manual for cleaning windows. Some windows are best cleaned by professional window cleaners. This book recommends reasonable and safe window cleaning practices (i.e. both feet on the ground and not leaning out a window). If this is not possible, then you should hire a professional window cleaner.

The author and publisher are not responsible for any damage that may occur to the property and any injury caused to a person or persons whatsoever. Also, there are no warranties, expressed or implied, concerning any products listed.

HOW TO CLEAN WINDOWS LIKE THE PROS
ISBN 0-9632123-3-8

FORMERLY TITLED
TAKING THE PANE OUT OF WINDOW CLEANING

SECOND PRINTING

PRINTED IN THE UNITED STATES OF AMERICA

Published by
Crystal Press
Simi Valley, CA

CONTENTS

Ugh! Streaks.

ACKNOWLEDGEMENTS

Writing a book is like pregnancy; it seems as though it will never end, especially during those hot summer months.

Organizing the typesetting, illustrations, editing, and printing are the labor and delivery of a book.

Once the "baby" is delivered, there is a sense of relief and joy, and I would like to thank those people who supported, helped, and encouraged me during my three year pregnancy.

Jim Dilts, the illustrator, whose excellent illustrations brought this book to life.

Lynn Bruton, for her editing skills.

Norm Popp, Santa Barbara Window Cleaning, and Steven Miller, Great Lakes Window Cleaning, for technical editing.

Karen Baxter, my wife, whose support and love made this book possible.

Thank You

INTRODUCTION

People spend thousands of dollars for new cars and take time to wash their windshields twice a week, but those same people will spend hundreds of thousands of dollars purchasing their homes and wash their windows once a year.

There is no reason they should tolerate admiring a gorgeous day through a grimy window. Window cleaning is simple. Modern day "good squeegees" are, with a little instruction, easy to use.

We all have a favorite window we like to view the world through. Maybe it's a bay window over the kitchen sink, a sliding glass door to the back yard, or a window with a special view. Learn to clean those one or two special windows you look through the most, and clean them once or twice a month.

Once you master the simplicity of window cleaning using the basic steps, everything else is just a song and a dance. Your confidence will grow and you may wish to experiment with "fanning the glass" or " high stick" work, making your window cleaning even faster and simpler.

Try window cleaning the way the professionals clean windows. The view outside your home will look much brighter.

IF A BLIND MAN CAN WASH A WINDOW...

T oby can't see, yet he still took the time to learn how to wash windows. He's slow moving and blends in with the glass and concrete structures. People on the sidewalks busy with their lives scurry by him all day long, never noticing his achievements.

He gently probes the window edge in front of him with a bony finger as he moves with a bucket and pole. After probing the wall for the windows' edge, he positions the bucket and pole against the wall but within reach. He reaches down into the soapy water for his wand and wrings the excess water from it before twisting it on to the pole. The twenty inches of glass in front of him are the hardest scrubbed in Los Angeles.

After dropping the wand into the bucket, he retrieves his squeegee from the belt holster and gives it a half twist onto the pole. He pulls the squeegee down to the window ledge directly in front of him three times, wiping the squeegee rubber each time. Then, he feels for the ledge and shuffles his feet ten inches to position himself in front of what wet window is left. When he's finished, the window sparkles and has not a streak.

If a blind man can wash windows, so can you.

> "A person's a failure only if he gives up trying."
> Toby

Channel

Rubber

T here are only five manufacturers of truly professional squeegees: ***Ettore, Unger, Sorbo, Pulex, and Mr. Longarm***. If you are not using a squeegee made by one of these manufacturers, then this book is a waste of your time and money. (See appendix for equipment you can purchase) Professional squeegee rubber undergoes constant testing for durability and wear. This highly technical rubber is precisely

Handle

molded and sliced using the strictest quality control. It's not easy making squeegee rubber that leaves a streakless window.

Manufacturers of professional window cleaning squeegees realize if the squeegee rubber they mold does not stand up to the expectations of professional window cleaners, they will be out of business.

Clean, streakless windows start with a professional squeegee.

STORAGE AND HANDLING

Professional window-cleaning squeegees need tender, loving care. Take care of them and they will provide you with years of streak-free windows.

So, when you are not using your squeegee:

1) Store it in a dark cool place. Rubber will deteriorate in light and dry air, causing the rubber's edge to be not as sharp and durable as it could be.

2) Store it with the rubber side facing up. Abrasions and nicks are caused during storage by the squeegee blade rubbing against a wall or shelf.

3) Clean and dry the squeegee before storing. Just like your dishes, it's a utensil to be cleaned and dried before putting away.

While you are using your squeegee:

1) Lay the squeegee down with the rubber side up. Don't risk scratching or nicking the rubber blade.

2) Lean the squeegee in a bucket so the metal, not the rubber, touches the side wall.

Always inspect the squeegee
before using it.

INSPECTING THE SQUEEGEE

Professional window cleaners always inspect the squeegee before working with it. Here is what to look for in your squeegee.

Rub your finger gently across the edge of the rubber. It should feel straight, not wavy or wrinkled. It should not feel stretched or tight.

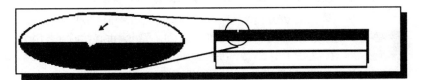

The tiniest nick in the rubber's edge, means a streak left on the window. If nicked, pull the rubber out and turn it around to use the other sharp edge.

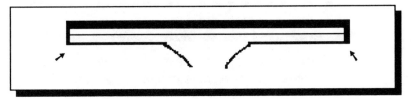

A 1/4 inch of rubber should stick out both ends of the squeegee. This is for softening the blow or to prevent scraping the paint off the window moldings.

The rubber should fit evenly in the squeegee's channel.

When you "bunch up" the rubber in the channel, it looks wavy in the channel. This causes the rubber not to lay flat against the window and will cause streaks.

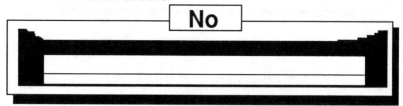

When you stretch the rubber the ends will appear raised and the middle taunt. This also causes the rubber not to lay flat against a window and causes streaks.

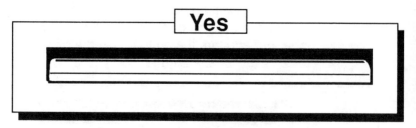

The rubber should look even from one end to the other. This will help minimize the streaks.

Check the pointed corners for wear. The squeegee rubber always begins to show wear at the corners first. They have a dull, rough look to them while the rest of it looks shiny and smooth. If a squeegee rubber has been used, you'll know it.

Looking from the side view

Inspect the squeegee for a bent or bowed channel. The channel should appear straight so even pressure will be applied to the rubber when you use it.

If the channel is bent, the rubber can't lay flat and will cause streaks on the window. When the channel is bowed, it has the same effect as being bent, except the streaks result from the center section of the channel. The rubber can't lay flat on the glass and consequently streaks are created.

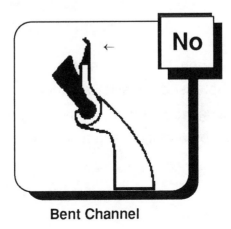

Bent Channel

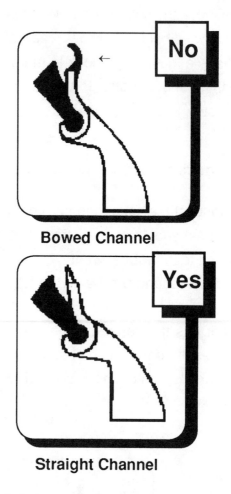

Bowed Channel

Straight Channel

When the channel is straight the rubber lays flat when pressed against a window. Get in the habit of inspecting your squeegee before you start. It will save you some frustration when you clean your windows.

SQUEEGEE HISTORY

I t is only in the last hundred years that squeegees for window cleaning existed. Before that time, glass was so irregular in smoothness that it was almost impossible to squeegee it. The first squeegee-type tools were used by Greek athletes around 500 B.C. They were fashioned out of gold or bronze and were used to scrape the oils and sweat from their

Squeegees in 500 B.C.

skin after athletic competitions. It was called an astregia.

The next we hear about squeegees is in the Middle Ages. Here is when the squeegee may have derived its modern name. A strip of leather was held together by two pieces of wood and attached to a pole. It made a "snakelike" movement when pushed across a deck of a boat. The name "squeilgee" may have been because of this "snakelike" movement or unusual sound it made as it scraped debris off the ship's deck.

A "squeilgee" around the Middle Ages

Around 1900, the first "modern" cleaning squeegee was invented. It was called the Chicago Squeegee, and was a thick strip of rubber between two thicker rubber strips bolted together with steel or brass. The rubber produced at that time was so irregular that window cleaners had to scrape it on the sidewalk to grind it down to a smooth edge.

The modern day squeegee was actually invented in 1936 by Ettore Steccone and consisted of a single strip of precision-cut rubber. It is still the basic tool of the professional window cleaning trade. In all, there are only five professional squeegee manufacturers in the world.

HOW SQUEEGEES WORK

When water is spread on a window most of it clings to the glass and will stay in place until you wipe it off or the sun dries it. Imagine those beads of water are small marbles spread evenly over a table.

If you had a 12 inch ruler to gather the marbles, you could move the ruler straight across the table and through the marbles. They would collect along the ruler's edge until the edge could hold no more.
Then... the marbles would begin to spill out each end of the ruler.

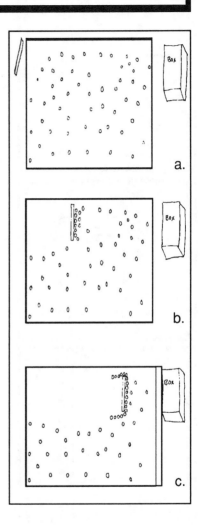

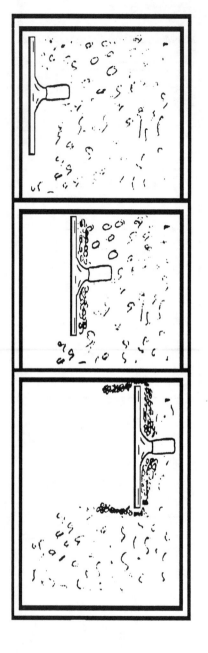

When you pull a squeegee across a window you collect the water beads under the squeegee channel, like collecting the marbles along the ruler.

As you continue to pull the squeegee across the glass, water continues to fill up the area behind the squeegee channel until...

the water overflows out both ends of the channel.

You want water to flow out one—not both—ends.

Similarly, if you squeegee down a window, you collect the water beads under the squeegee channel (like collecting the marbles along the ruler.)

As you continue to pull the squeegee down the window, water continues to fill up the area under the squeegee channel until...

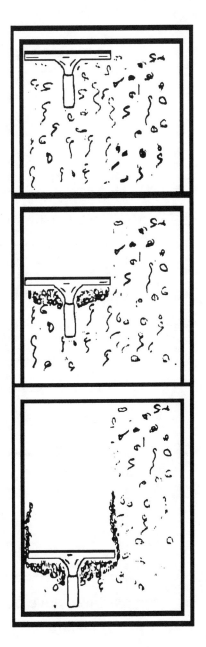

the water overflows out both ends of the channel.

Again, you want water to flow out one end but not both ends.

With the marbles spread on the table,

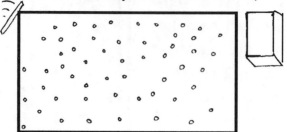

if you turn the ruler slightly

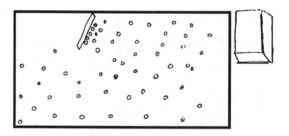

and then move through the marbles

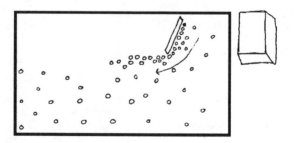

the marbles move out the side of
"least resistance."

Each time you pull through the marbles...

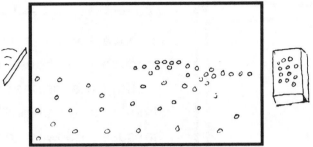

keep the ruler at the same angle.

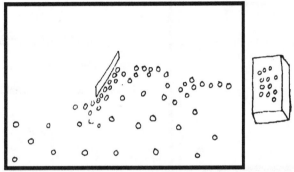

The marbles will flow to the easiest side to escape.

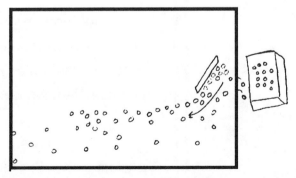

Eventually, you will clear all the marbles without having to go back for a single one.

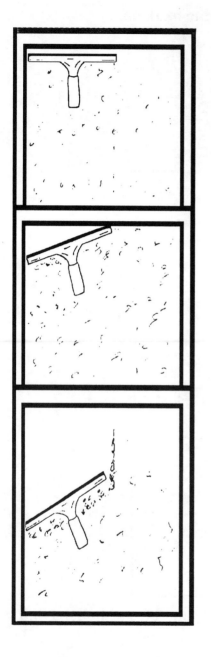

The trick to using a squeegee successfully is to move the water in a direction you choose by angling the squeegee slightly. If you are pulling the squeegee down the window...

turn one side (so one side of the channel is lower than the other).

As you move the squeegee down the wet window, the water builds up under the channel and...

water flows out the easiest side – **the side of _least resistance_.**

When you position the squeegee next to the dry area you just finished...

turn your squeegee to the same angle as the first stroke down the glass.

Squeegee down the glass, keeping the angle the same all the way down.

The water will continue to flow to the higher side — the side of *least resistance.*

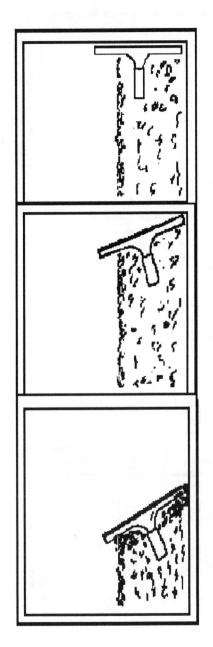

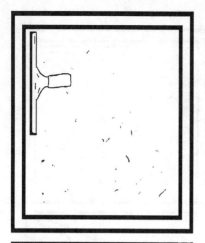

The same principle applies when pulling the squeegee across the glass.

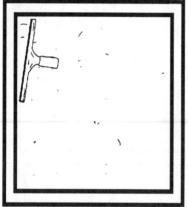

Angle the squeegee top half ahead of the bottom half.

As you pull the squeegee straight across the glass the water builds up underneath the channel. The water flows out the lower end of the squeegee. It's the easiest side to leave, the side of *"least resistance"*.

When you position the squeegee next to the dry area you just finished...

angle the squeegee top half ahead of the bottom half.

The water continues to move down the lower sections of the glass, the side of *"least resistance"*

These are the two basic laws of window cleaning.

Across the glass, the top half of the squeegee leads the bottom half.

Down the glass, one squeegee side (the dry side) is lower than the other side.

Sometimes your equipment has a mind of its own.

THE 10 WINDOW CLEANING COMMANDMENTS

Before you start cleaning windows, there are a few commandments regarding the use of the squeegee. These rules hold true if you are learning the basic pull across – pull down window cleaning, or the more advanced continuous motion window cleaning (fanning).

Take the time to review all ten commandments. The better you understand these principles, the fewer the streaks, the less time it will take, and the easier window cleaning will be.

COMMANDMENT ONE
Change the squeegee rubber often.

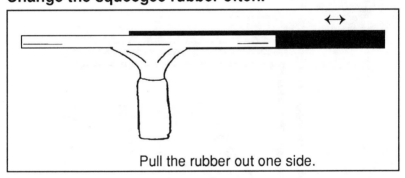

Pull the rubber out one side.

Squeegee rubber worn out by repeated use will cause streaks and frustrate you. The rubber should be changed after 15 hours of use or sooner, if necessary. Professional window cleaning rubber is easily purchased from the sources listed in the back of the book.

COMMANDMENT TWO
Relax your hand, wrist, and arm.

Gripping the
squeegee tightly
while window
cleaning will
exhaust you
quickly.

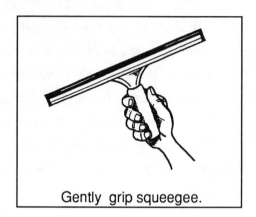

Gently grip squeegee.

COMMANDMENT THREE
Angle the squeegee to channel the water.

Don't forget the two inch overlap.

Remember, water moves to the side of *least resistance*.

COMMANDMENT FOUR

Use fingers and wrist for squeegee movement.

If you notice
your arm, elbow,
shoulder, or your
whole body moving
around you are
working too hard.
The action is all in
the wrist and fingers.

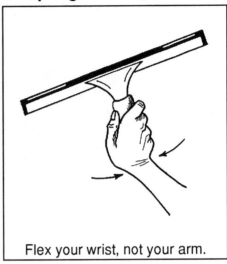

Flex your wrist, not your arm.

COMMANDMENT FIVE

Start the squeegee at the edge of the window, not in the middle of the window.

| Start from the edge. | Not from the middle. |

COMMANDMENT SIX
Squeegee with gentle pressure on the glass.

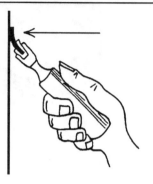

Light pressure is all that is needed when squeegeeing a window.   Anything else is working too hard.

RELAX – WINDOW CLEANING IS FUN!

COMMANDMENT SEVEN
Squeegee without stopping in the middle .

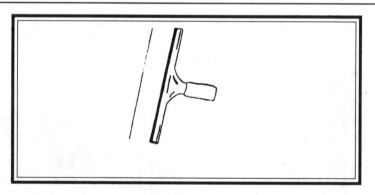

Starting, then stopping and starting again leaves
window streaks. Start from one edge and glide in one
continuous stroke to the other edge.

COMMANDMENT EIGHT
Overlap at least 2 inches of dry glass.

Water builds up under the channel as you move the squeegee. Even with the squeegee angled properly, water could spill out the wrong end unless you overlap at least 2 inches of dry glass.

Two inch overlap.

COMMANDMENT NINE
Position the squeegee handle close to the glass so that your knuckles are about an inch away from the glass.

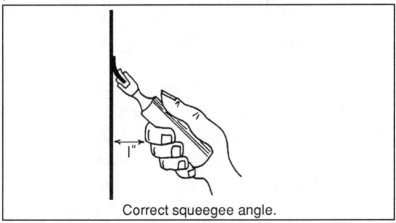

Correct squeegee angle.

COMMANDMENT TEN

Wipe the rubber's edge occasionally with the sponge.

Wipe with your damp sponge.

OR, Tap the squeegee gently, in the window area that is still wet.

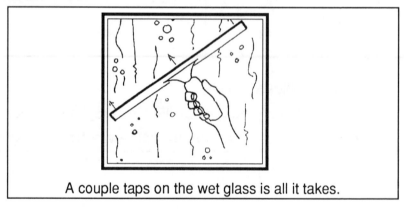

A couple taps on the wet glass is all it takes.

You need to remove excess water, dirt, lint, or other foreign matter trapped under the rubber. You would be surprised by the number of streaks made because of a piece of lint or hair caught on the rubber.

Follow these simple few rules and window cleaning will be much more rewarding and fun!

WASHING THE WINDOW

Washing the window properly before squeegeeing it can save you headaches and frustration when you do squeegee.

Most professionals use Joy or Dawn dishwashing liquid soap. It doesn't leave a film on the window and leaves a nice shine on the glass. There are some dish soaps that are as good, but try different soaps and see which you like best. Dishwashing soap is the quickest, simplest, and safest window cleaning solution and one that is already available in your home.

Use as much as you would normally use to wash your dishes – enough to get the windows clean, but not so much that you get soap foam in your bucket or sink.

Your local janitorial supply store should have a number of window cleaning solutions to choose from if you wish to purchase a stronger or more concentrated one.

You want a cleaner that not only helps remove grease and dirt, but also helps the squeegee glide easily across the glass and preserve the rubber longer.

"Our boss is so paranoid that people will find out we use JOY Dishwashing detergent to wash windows, he makes us put it into an unmarked bottle." — A window cleaner.

Here are a few cleaners favored by professionals that you may wish to add to your liquid soap and water.
Ammonia

Ammonia has been household favorite for years. There is nothing terribly wrong with it. You add an an ounce of ammonia to the soap in your bucket

TSP (Trisodium Phosphate)

This powder is sometimes added to a window cleaning solution for extra cleaning action. You add just an ounce of the powder to your soap and water. But, it is terribly hard on your hands.

HINT

Rubbing Alcohol
Window cleaners sometime put rubbing alcohol in a spray bottle and use it to wash windows, especially French windows. It works well on smudges and fingerprints, plus it leaves no residue on the glass since it evaporates in a short time.

Warning: Whatever you decide to use, read all manufacturers directions and recommendations carefully before using their products. Be careful not to inhale fumes and airborne cleaning particles.

Squeegeeing the glass without a soapy solution is like shaving yourself with only water." — A window cleaner.

WETTING THE WINDOW

You can hold your water in a variety of containers. If you have only one or two windows to clean just rinse your wand under a faucet and squirt a little dish soap on one side of the wand. You can also wet a small clean rag under a faucet, squirt a little dish soap on it and scrub the window. If you have more than a couple windows to clean you can use the following to hold water:

The kitchen sink

A bucket

A spray bottle

A utility tray

Tools you use for wetting the window include many household items.

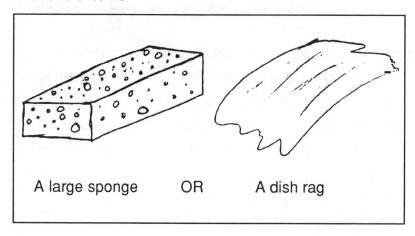

A large sponge   OR   A dish rag

Tools you can use that a professional works with include:

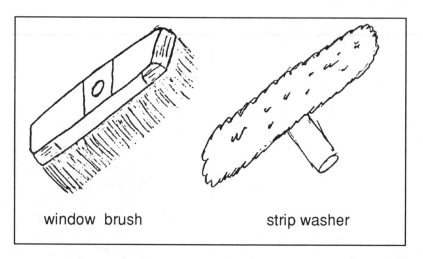

window brush   strip washer

The strip washer (commonly called a wand) is the preferred wetting tool of the professional window cleaner.

If you are serious about clean windows a wand is a must. (See the appendix for more information on how to order one today.)

Here are a few tips for wetting the window.

Squirt the soap on the sponge, rag, or wand instead of in the water, then rinse the sponge, rag, or wand in the bucket water or under a faucet a few times.

Applying the soap directly to the washing tool will give you a greater concentration of cleaning action where you need it most.

Squeeze the excess water out before applying rag or sponge to the window.

The inside windows need less water. There is less dirt and grit on the interior side — mostly dust. Besides, the less water you use, the less that can fall on the carpet. Use as little water and soap as necessary. Use more water only when you are cleaning extra dusty, dirty windows (like the exterior). Or, if you are cleaning glass that is hot from the sunlight.

Caution: Stay away from abrasive pads. They can scratch widows.

Develop a pattern for wetting a window, one that feels comfortable to you. A sample pattern is depicted below.

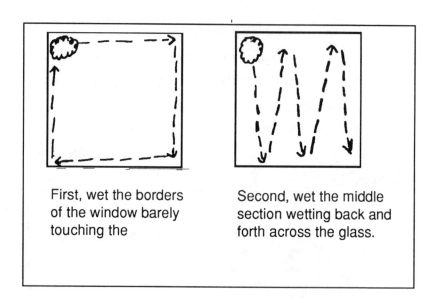

First, wet the borders of the window barely touching the

Second, wet the middle section wetting back and forth across the glass.

Wet the entire window including the corners. People tend to miss the corners when wetting the window, causing smears when you squeegee it.

Wet the top and sides of the window carefully. Use a "side to side" motion while barely touching the moldings.

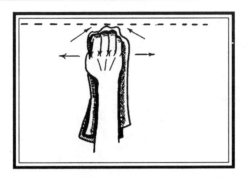

Up and down motions that "bang" into the top window molding push water underneath the molding that drips out later. (Sometimes this is called a "crying window" because it looks like tears.)

HINT

When washing hot windows use extra water or colder water to help keep the water from evaporating too fast.

When washing extra dirty and dusty windows use extra water to help flush the dirt off the window.

Practice these methods of washing a window. Each one helps to prevent streaking or smearing after you use the squeegee. They are an important part of window cleaning.

Next time bring the ladder!

HOW TO SQUEEGEE

Now is the moment of truth. This is just the basic technique of window cleaning. Remember to practice on windows that are not tinted. Be kind to yourself. We strive for streak free windows, but nobody is perfect, including professional window cleaners. If you have streaky windows when you finish, refer to the "Trouble Shooting" section. To help minimize streaking go ahead and use your towel to wipe away about 1/2 inch along the top and side edge of the glass surface before you squeegee.

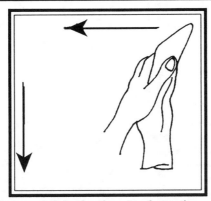

Wipe a 1/2 inch of water from the edge before you squeegee.

HINT

Hold your wand or sponge directly under the squeegee to catch the water dripping off the rubber while squeegeeing.

43

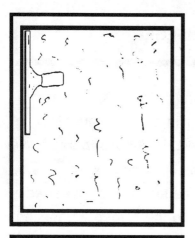

Squeegeeing across a window

If you start from the left corner...

glide all the way across without stopping. The top half of the squeegee should be ahead of the bottom half.

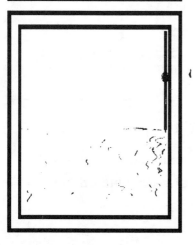

When you get to the other side, pull up slightly on the handle and pull the squeegee to the window's edge. To remove excess water from the rubber, wipe the rubber once or twice with your sponge. Or, tap the rubber once or twice on the wet glass.

Then...

Start from the side. Remember to overlap two inches of dry glass.

Glide across the window, the top half of the squeegee ahead of the bottom half.

When you get to the other side, pull up slightly on the handle and pull the squeegee to the window's edge. If streaks appear, see the Trouble Shooting section. There might be some water left on the sides. Use your dry "lintless" rag to wipe down the sides. Certain rags may leave streaks and smudges, so test them.

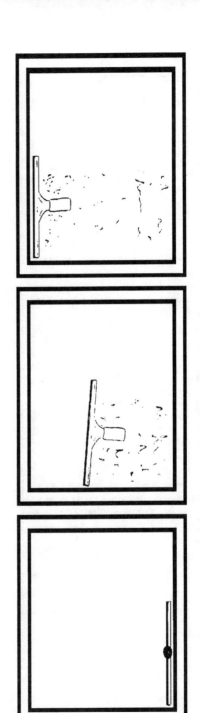

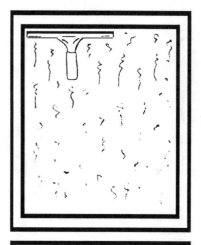

Squeegeeing down a window

If you start from the left side:

Angle the squee-gee so the water flows toward the wet side of the window.

Glide the squee-gee, without stopping, to the bottom and...

lift the handle away from the window so the squeegee rubber can reach the bottom of the glass.

Remove the ex-cess. **It seems so simple because it is so simple.**

Remove the excess water from the rubber by wiping the rubber once with your sponge, or tapping the rubber once on wet glass.

Start at the top, next to the dry glass you just squee-geed. Overlap two inches of dry glass.

Glide down the window, angling the squeegee so the water flows to the side of least resistance toward the wet side (even if you are next to the molding on the other side.)

When you get to the ledge, pull up slightly on the handle and pull the squeegee to the bottom of the window.

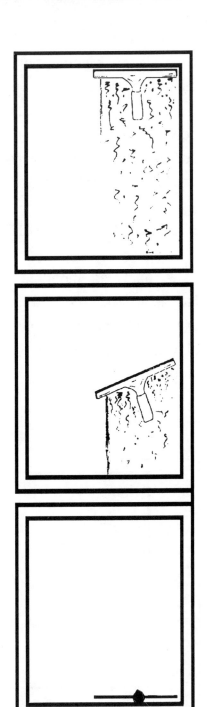

If the window moldings or ledges are making it difficult to squeegee the whole window, then squeegee as far as you can across and then squeegee the last stroke down the window. There may by a tiny section of window still wet. Use your dry, lintless towel or chamois to wipe it dry. Remember to practice.

LEDGES ARE IMPORTANT

Just as important as clean windows are clean ledges or sills. After you finish squeegeeing the window, wipe the ledges and, if necessary, the wall right away. If dirty water is left on the ledge, it will eventually stain the ledge. So, with a sponge, wipe that ledge NOW.

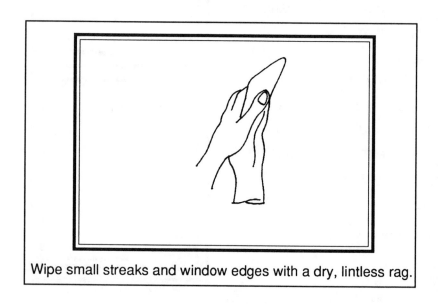

Wipe small streaks and window edges with a dry, lintless rag.

TROUBLE SHOOTING

Lines or smears of water left on the glass after cleaning are called streaks. RELAX, everyone has trouble with streaks, even professional window cleaners. The solution is knowing what causes streaks on windows. There are many reasons and I have categorized them for easy reference to help you prevent streaks in the future.

THE PROBLEM: A streak line or lines appear as you move the squeegee across the window.

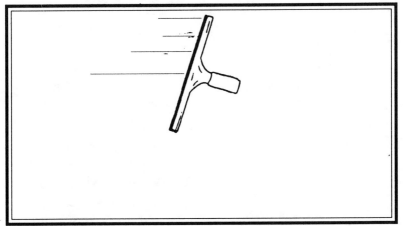

POSSIBLE REASON

SOLUTION

Lint or dirt
caught between
the rubber and
the window preventing
the rubber laying
flat against the surface.

Wipe the rubber with
your sponge or rag.
Do this at regular
intervals.

POSSIBLE REASON	SOLUTION
There is a nick or cut in the rubber.	Rub your finger the length of the rubber's edge. Feel for the tiniest nick or cut. If you find one, turn the rubber around or replace the rubber.
The rubber is old and worn.	Look at the front edge of the rubber. If it looks scratched and dull, particularly the corners, it's time to replace the rubber.
The window isn't wet enough for the amount of dirt on the glass.	If the water on the window is muddy looking, the grains of dirt might be catching the rubber when you squeegee. Wash the window again, using extra water to flush the excess dirt from the window.
The water has dried on the glass.	Look for glass partly dry. You can't squeegee drying glass. Squeaking noises when you squeegee are a sure sign of drying glass. Wet the window again.

POSSIBLE REASON	SOLUTION
The rubber you are using is not of professional quality.	Ettore, Sorbo, Unger, and Pulex are the only professional quality squeegee rubbers.
The rubber is not straight in the channel. Channel is bent or bowed.	See the chapter on "Storage and Handling".
The squeegee handle is too far from the window.	If your knuckles are more than an inch from the glass, they are too far. Bring the handle closer to the window.
Soapy water build-up on the back of the rubber and channel.	Inspect the back of the channel and the rubber for excess soapy water. Wipe off any excess.
Excess soap and foam in the water.	Look in your bucket for soap foam. An inch or more is too much. Fill again with clean water.
The window moldings are too wet.	When you squeegee the edge and have streaks longer than two inches, the edges of the moldings and glass are too wet. Wipe the area where the glass and moldings meet.

THE PROBLEM: A streak appears at the end of the squeegee.

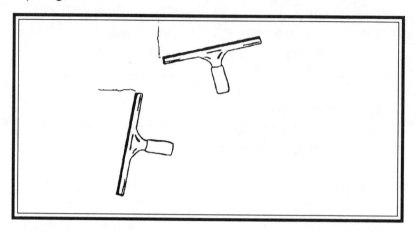

POSSIBLE REASON | SOLUTION

Too much water on the rubber

If you have squeegeed one or two passes down or across the glass, you should wipe the squeegee once with the sponge or rag. Better yet, just tap the rubber on what glass is still wet to shake off the water – it's much faster.

The end of the rubber is raised up in the channel.

Look at the front edge of the rubber. If the ends are raised even slightly it can cause streaking. Make sure the rubber is smooth and flat in the channel.

POSSIBLE REASON	SOLUTION
The squeegee isn't tilted to channel the water properly.	The squeegee needs to be angled to channel the water off the window properly. (See "How a Squeegee Works" on page 19.)
There is too much water being squeegeed and not enough dry glass at one end when you squeegee.	While you squeegee, look at the area being squeegeed. If it is all water along the rubber it's too much for the squeegee too handle. Except for the first pass on the glass, all squeegee strokes across or down the window should include approximately two inches of dry glass. (See Commandment Eight "overlap 2 inches").

THE PROBLEM: Short and long streaks are formed from where the squeegee started at the window's edge.

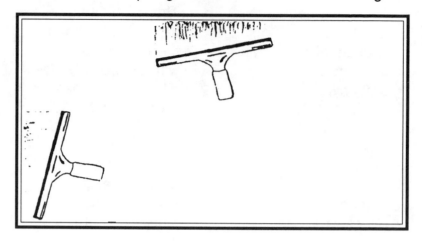

POSSIBLE REASON	SOLUTION
The window molding and glass edge are too wet.	Excessive water at the window's edge won't allow you to squeegee cleanly. Use a dry cloth or damp sponge and wipe the window's edge.
The squeegee rubber has too much water on it.	If you have squeegeed two passes down, or across the glass, you should wipe the squeegee once with the sponge. Better yet, just tap the rubber on what glass is still wet to shake off the water– it's much faster.

THE PROBLEM: Diagonal streaks appear near the sides or middle of the window.

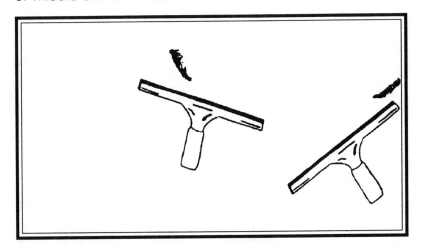

POSSIBLE REASON	SOLUTION
Squeegee channel bumped the molding.	If the end of the squeegee bumps the molding too hard at the end of the stroke, it raises the rubber leaking water on the dry glass.
While turning the squeegee on the window, you raised the higher side of the channel enough to leak water under the rubber.	When using the "fanning" style, make sure you keep equal pressure on both sides of the handle.

THE PROBLEM: Streaks that look like "arrowheads" appear near the end of the stroke.

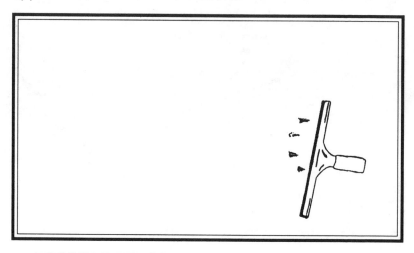

POSSIBLE REASON

You have extra
dusty windows
that require
you use more
water.

The rubber is
worn out and
needs replacing.

SOLUTION

The rubber is prevented
from laying flat on the
glass because of extra
dusty grit on the glass
Use more water and
wet the window again.
Flush off as much dirt
as possible.

Look at the front edge
of the rubber. If it
looks scratched and
dull, particularly the
corners, it's time to
replace the rubber.

THE PROBLEM: Thick, wobbly looking streak lines or V
shaped wobbly-looking streak lines.

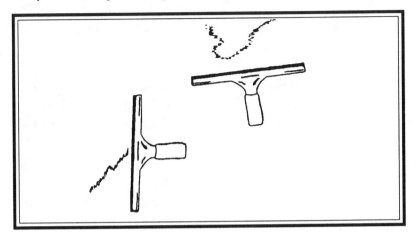

POSSIBLE REASON

Pressing harder
on one side of
the squeegee
than the other.

SOLUTION

Squeegee pressure on
the window should be
equal on both sides
of the handle. Certain
twisting of your wrist
will cause more
pressure to be exerted
on one side of the
channel, lifting
the other side off
the glass.
Put the same amount of
pressure on both sides
as you glide the
squeegee on the
window.

POSSIBLE REASON	SOLUTION
The water had dried before being squeegeed.	Make sure the glass is wet. You can't squeegee dry glass.
Squeegee angle becoming too sharp.	Keep your knuckles about an inch off the window till the end of the stroke. Moving your hand away from the window decreases the amount of rubber area squeegeeing the glass.
No pressure on the glass with the squeegee.	Are you pulling the squeegee off the glass as you glide across the window? Maintain equal pressure the length of the stroke.

THE PROBLEM: The water solution just smears on the window.

POSSIBLE REASON

SOLUTION

The water had
dried before
being squeegeed.

You can't squeegee
a dried window. Even a
partially dried window
will streak. If the
window is drying up,
wet again the area that's
dried and begin again.

The entire window
surface wasn't
washed properly.

People tend to miss
wetting the corners or
a large strip of glass
along the top of a
window. When you
squeegee the area, it
smears the dirt with the
little water that's on
the rubber. Wash
the entire window.

THE PROBLEM: A streak line the length of the squee-gee appears.

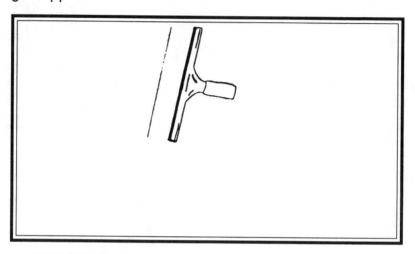

POSSIBLE REASON	SOLUTION
You are starting to squeegee in the middle of the window.	The squeegee should be started from one of the window sides. If you start from within the glass you will get a line at the starting point.
You are hesitating the squeegee in the middle of the stroke.	If you start the squeegee, then stop, then continue the stroke, you will get a line the length of your squeegee. You can go slower — you just can't stop.

THE PROBLEM: A series of bar streaks appear on one side of the squeegee when squeegeeing the window.

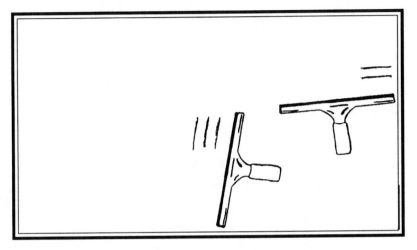

POSSIBLE REASON

Too much dry
glass overlap and
not enough wet glass
being squeegeed,
causing the
squeegee to
vibrate slightly.

The squeegee and
window molding
are rubbing
causing friction.

SOLUTION

You should squeegee
two inches of dry
window on each
succeeding pass after
the first one. Four
inches or more of dry
glass along the
squeegee channel and
the rubber on the dry
glass will produce
friction and vibrate up
off the window.

Touch the moldings
with the squeegee.
Don't press against
them.

THE PROBLEM: Water drips down from the top molding. This is called a "crying window" because it looks like tears.

POSSIBLE REASON	SOLUTION
Water pushed under molding when window was washed.	When you push a rag, sponge, or wand up against a window's top molding, you are pushing the water underneath the molding. It will stay there until gravity pulls it out and down the window. Wash the top molding using a side-to-side motion, barely touching the molding.

HARD TO REACH FIRST FLOOR WINDOWS

Many ground floor windows are either too tall, too high, or have too many obstructions such as bushes or couches in the way. For these reasons, we use a pole or a ladder to reach the unreachable. We also use a pole to reach windows to the side of us as well.

All the window commandments for cleaning high windows are the same as for lower windows. There is one additional rule regarding pole work, and it is the most important. When the pole is not in use, lean it close-up against a wall, out of the way. Never lay it on the ground. Someone, including yourself, may trip on it.

Never lay your pole on the ground.

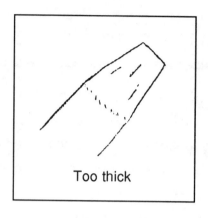
Too thick

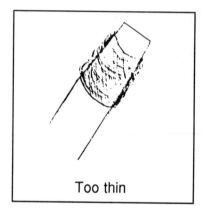
Too thin

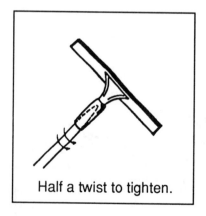
Half a twist to tighten.

THE POLE

Most high first-floor window cleaning can be done with the help of an ordinary pole, about the size of a broom handle.

If the pole you own is too thick for your squeegee, carefully whittle a small amount of wood off one end.

If the wood pole you own is too thin, causing the squeegee or wand to fit loosely or fall off, then wrap a thick tape around one end. Electrician's tape or duct tape is good. Use enough tape to wrap once around the pole end or until the squeegee fits snugly.

A squeegee needs a half a twist to get it to fit snugly on the pole.

EXTENSION POLES

You can also purchase a more sophisticated extension pole with adjustable sections that slide to different lengths. These poles are made in lengths ranging from two feet to 45 feet. Poles over 12 feet in length can become unmanageable for the homeowner. With practice, though, you can become as skilled as a professional window cleaner.

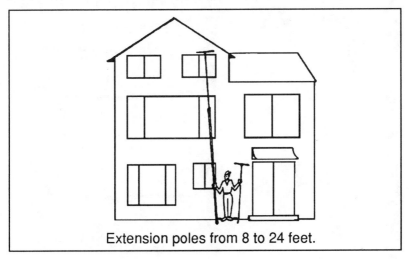

Extension poles from 8 to 24 feet.

If by chance your extension pole has a metal protrusion that looks like a screw and your squeegee just spins on the top, buy a tapered wood head that will screw on to the pole and fit your squeegee

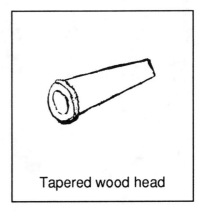

Tapered wood head

THE STRIPWASHER

The best and most common tool for wetting windows that are out of reach is the stripwasher, commonly called "the wand". I strongly recommend the purchase of one if you have windows that are out of reach. A wand will make the job of window wetting much easier. (See the appendix to purchase one.)

A wand also fits on the end of a broom pole or an extension pole. It can fit loosely or snugly on an extension pole.

The most common mistakes beginners make are:

1) Not wetting the entire window, especially the top. They miss one or two inches of the top portion of the window so when they squeegee a dirty window it drags the dirt down the window as smears.
2) Wetting too much window area at one time, causing evaporation before it can be squeegeed.
3) Waiting too long before squeegeeing a drying window.

Now that you know what to look out for, here are a few hints to help your pole work even more.

1) Use more water on the exterior windows. They are usually dustier and require more water to help squeegee all that excess dust and dirt.
2) If you are using an extension pole with multiple sections, extend the bottom sections first. It will keep that section of the pole closest to the wand stiffer and that will give you more pressure for scrubbing the window.
3) Don't wash the higher windows in the direct sunlight or on windy days. It can be done but at this point it will frustrate you.

WETTING THE WINDOW

When wetting a high window, use the same principles as wetting one that you can reach. Wet the window starting at the top. Move the wand back and forth across the top of the glass.

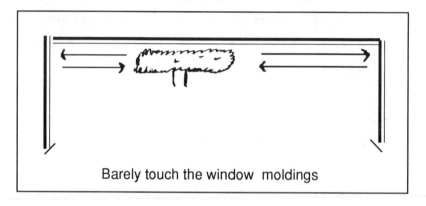
Barely touch the window moldings

Now, move the wand up and down as you move across the window, wetting the window no lower than your shoulders.

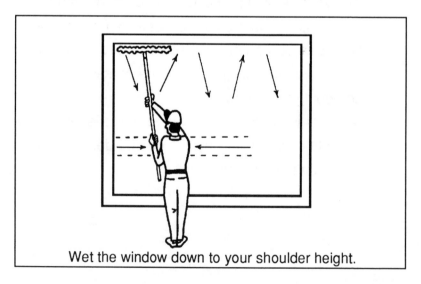
Wet the window down to your shoulder height.

As you wash the window, all the exercise should be in your arm motions. Your back should not have to move at all. You are washing the top half of the window first.

SQUEEGEEING THE WINDOW

Squeegeeing high windows uses the same technique learned when we squeegeed down a window.

Squeegee down to shoulder height and remember to angle the squeegee so the water flows toward the wet side.

Remove the excess water on the squeegee by:

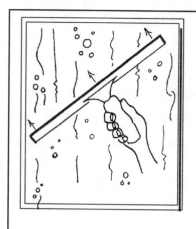 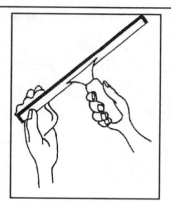

tapping the squeegee
lightly on the
wet side of the   OR
window.

wiping the squeegee
off with a rag or
sponge.

When you finish the upper section of the window, take the squeegee off the pole. Scrub the lower section making sure you get the corners.

Start from the window side and remember to overlap two inches of dry glass.

If you notice water marks   left on the glass, check the "Trouble Shooting" section for help.

The top edge may have water that the squeegee did not get, and these splotches of water may begin to dribble down.

Place your clean lintfree rag on the end of your pole and wipe the top edge. The longer you wait to wipe the top edge, the greater the chance of water dripping down.

Pole work, like regular window cleaning, takes practice. It can be frustrating at times. But, with persistence and practice you can become a pro.

It's Showtime!

"FANNING" WITH A SQUEEGEE

F anning the window with the squeegee means to clean the glass without lifting the squeegee off the glass, thus squeegeeing the entire window in one motion. Sometimes this is called the "swirl", the "S" style, or "snaking it". In fact, many window cleaners do not consider someone a window cleaner unless he or she can " fan" a window. (That's pure hogwash, so don't worry about it.)

The two basic principles of window cleaning are still at work when we "fan" the glass. Our hands and wrists do most of the work.

The pattern is to move back and forth across the glass, moving the water down the glass as you clean.

The trick is to keep it moving by using your fingers and wrist to turn the squeegee around on the glass.

It's not a stiff motion. The tendency for most people is to lock their hand around the squeegee and use their elbow and shoulder to turn the squeegee. If you find your elbow and shoulder moving around while you are squeegeeing, then you are working too hard.

There is a better way – it's all in the wrist and fingers.

PRACTICING THE FANNING TECHNIQUE

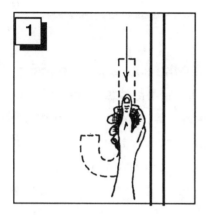

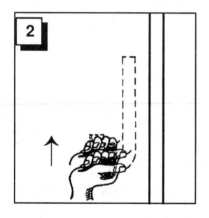

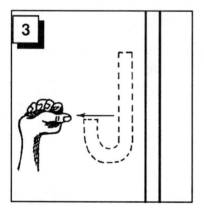

The toughest part about fanning is the turn at either side of the window. To help ensure you make the turn correctly, practice the turning without the squeegee. The turn is similar to writing the letter "J" with your knuckles on the right side of the window and a backwards "J" on the left side of the window. Press your knuckles lightly against a window with your palm facing toward the center of the window.

1) Glide your knuckles down the window about 12 inches.

2) As you turn at the bottom of the "J", twist your wrist so that the palm of your hand faces upward.

3) When you finish outlining the letter "J", move your knuckles across the glass to the window edge on the

other side. This last step is the start across to the other side. Glide across the window till your knuckles touch the window molding on the other side.

Turn your wrist so the palm of your hand faces the window's edge.

1) Start outlining a backwards letter "J" on the glass.

2) As you turn at the bottom of the backwards letter "J", twist your wrist till the palm of your hand faces the ground.

3) When you finish the outline, pull your knuckles back across the glass to the other side and outline a letter "J" on that side again.

The trick is moving smoothly with no stopping.

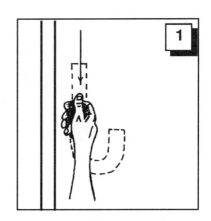

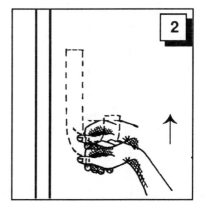

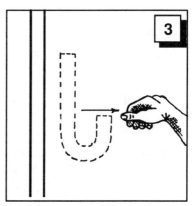

THE COMPLETE MOTION OF FANNING A WINDOW

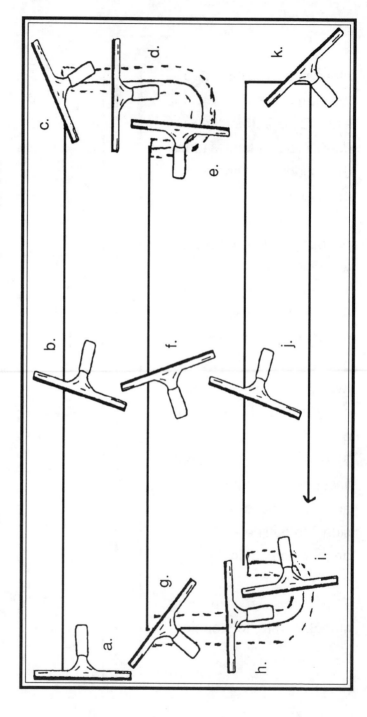

FANNING THE WINDOW

These squeegee moves on the glass are all one smooth motion that squeegees the entire window. Press the squeegee lightly on the window. It will help you in the turns. Use your wrist and fingers to turn the squeegee around on the glass—not your arm and shoulder.

If you were to drive a car and turn right into your driveway, you would not stop the car and turn the steering wheel and then start up the driveway. In one smooth easy motion you would keep the car moving forward as you turn the steering wheel.

a) Start in the top left corner of the window.

b) Pull the squeegee across the glass as you normally would with the top half of the channel ahead of the bottom half.

c) Notice the turn has begun before you touch squeegee channel's end in the corner of the window.

d) Pull the squeegee down the glass starting the letter "J". As you squeegee down the window make sure the end of the squeegee channel is touching the side of the window. This downward move is the beginning of your turn.

e) At the bottom of the "J", twist your wrist and move it up at the same angle as pictured (as you practiced on the last page). When you finish the "J", pull the squeegee back across the glass. (Remember to use your fingers and wrist to turn the squeegee, not your arm, elbow, or shoulder.

f) Pull the squeegee across the glass with the top of the squeegee ahead of the bottom.

g) Start to angle the squeegee more so that when you touch the molding you can start the backwards "J" down the window more easily.

h) Start down the window.

i) When you get to the bottom of your back-wards "J", twist your wrist so your palm faces down. Keep moving up the "J". When you finish, start across the window.

j) Going back across the window, keep the top half ahead of the bottom half.

k) When you can't make a figure "J" on the glass anymore, just keep the squeegee end against the molding and pull across it the bottom.

TORQUEING THE SQUEEGEE

Torqueing the squeegee means twisting your wrist so that pressure is applied to only one side of the squeegee. Up to now we have applied equal pressure to both sides of the channel.

Occasionally, water remains on the glass on the farthest right or farthest left three inches of window. Maybe the surface of the glass has a depression or the squeegee channel is bent and the squeegee rubber glides over it leaving a little pool of wetness instead of a clean window. You torque the squeegee to finish the cleaning.

To do this you need extra pressure on one side of the squeegee and you accomplish this by twisting your wrist.

This twisting motion to the left or right side of the squeegee presses the squeegee rubber down on one channel side and lifts the opposite channel side slightly.

HOW TO DO IT

With a firm grip around the squeegee, twist your hand as though your knuckles are trying to reach the window. You will see the squeegee rubber flatten out on the side pressure is being exerted on. You will also feel the pressure exerted on the side of the squeegee.

To put pressure on the other side, twist your hand as though the palm of your hand is trying to touch the window. You will see the rubber flatten on the window.

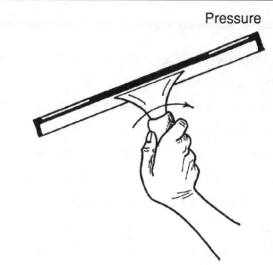

Pressure

Twisting the handle to the right increases pressure on the right side of the squeegee channel.

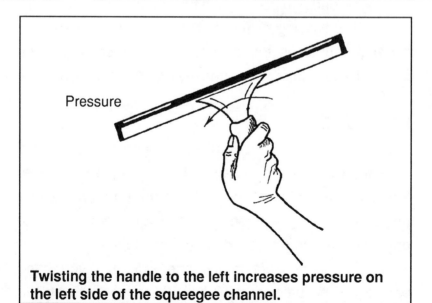

Pressure

Twisting the handle to the left increases pressure on the left side of the squeegee channel.

Torqueing the squeegee to clean excess water away from the edge is easier and faster.

Twist your wrist to the right so only a few inches of channel touches the glass. Glide the squeegee across the top.

Twist your wrist to the left so only a few inches of channel touch the glass on the left side. Glide along the left window's edge top to bottom.

Now tap the wet glass to shake off the excess water and begin your usual squeegee strokes.

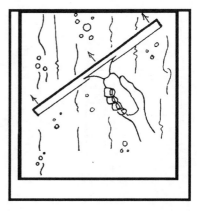

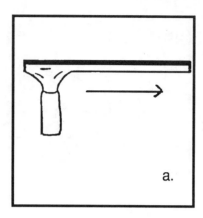

a.

b.

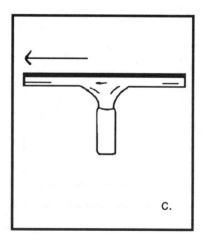

c.

When the top of the window is just out of reach, use the torqueing method.

Instead of using a pole when the window is only inches out of reach, either above or to the side of you, torque the squeegee with the channel extended completely to one side.

a. Loosen the channel and pull it to the right. You want all the channel to one side but enough left in the handle to still hold it firmly.

b. Torque the squeegee to the all-channel side and glide across the top to the other side.

c. When you don't have to reach anymore, loosen the handle and slide the channel back to its original position.

82

French windows

French windows

French windows are small window panes grouped together in sets of 4,6,8,9,10,12,or15 panes in a door or window. (Sometimes they are called "cut ups".) If the squeegee is too big for the window, you can cut the squeegee down to size with a hack saw (or see the order form in the appendix for different size channels you can order.

Cleaning French windows is simple.

1) Use a damp sponge or rag to wet the window, wetting in a square (not circular) motion. Wet 3 or 4 window panes at a time.

2) Take a dry towel and clean off the top and left edge of the glass. (Put your

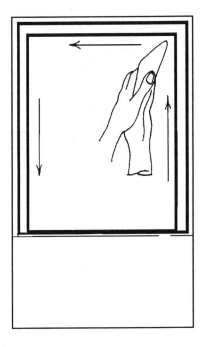

finger in the towel and wipe 1/2 inch of glass).

3) Squeegee across the window and wipe the rubber, then squeegee again. Cleaning four windows at a time should not be a problem.

Irregular windows

Windows come in many different shapes. The trick to squeegeeing them is to start at the lower end when pulling the squeegee down the window so your squeegee is properly angled from the start. When going across the window start at the higher side and follow the angle as you glide across the glass.

Louvered Windows

Louvered Windows are those long, rectangular

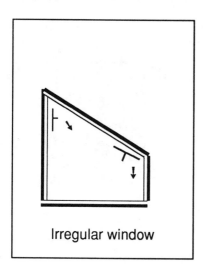

Irregular window

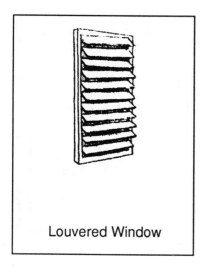

Louvered Window

glass panes set parallel to one another that open and close like a shutter. What a pain in the neck. To clean them, first open them as far as they will go. Start at the top louver, and wet the top and bottom with a wet rag or sponge. Extra water on the top side will be necessary because of the excess dirt.

Now squeegee the top of the first louver length ways. Turn over the squeegee and glide across the bottom side. It will look imperfect. Louvers are difficult and demand patience.

MIRRORS

Many people see cleaning mirrors as being different from windows. In reality, you utilize the same window cleaning techniques. Wash and squeegee the mirrors just as you would an ordinary window, but do watch out for electrical outlets.

CAUTION: Many mirrors have electrical plug outlets protruding from their surface. Take precautions not to get the plug outlet wet and electrocute yourself or start a fire.

TINTED WINDOWS

There are many types of laminated plastics "wallpapered" to windows. They decrease the sun's heat and glare into a home or car.

Most laminated tint is easily scratched. To lessen these noticeable lines, what you use to wet the window is extremely important. Never use razor blades or rough cloths or rough pads on a tinted window. They will scratch the tint.

The best washing cloths are old soft 100% cotton T-shirts or soft baby diapers. Soft sponges are also acceptable (meaning sponges that are soft even when dry).

After you wet the window, use the two-step method to squeegee the window . Fanning the glass may scratch the tint.

Stickers and tape adhering to a tinted window can be a "sticky" problem. There is a product called "Remove it" that loosens the tape glue enough to allow for easy removal.

CAUTION: With the many varieties of window tinting available today, it is recommended that you ask a window tinting professional in your area any further questions you may have regarding tinted windows. If a squeegee is acceptable, please squeegee to your heart's content.

STORM WINDOWS

Regular sliding windows that also include a removable outer glass plate are sometimes called "storm" windows. In climates that reach below freezing temperatures and are subject to violent weather changes, homes are equipped with these removable panes. During the hot summer months, they can be removed and stored and before winter, the storm windows are usually cleaned and then put on the exterior side of the window.

THERMALPANE WINDOWS

A Thermalpane window, like storm windows, has an insulating air space between two panes of glass. While storm window panes are removeable, the thermalpane windows are fabricated together and can not come apart. Thermalpane windows clean just like regular windows except you don't want to use razor blades against the edges. The air space is sealed between the two panes. If there is a leak into the air space, moisture leaks in and fogs the window. Using razor blades near the edges may break the seal.

CAR WINDOWS

The twelve inch squeegee is great for car windows. The trick is to follow the curves of the glass so the squeegee rubber will lay flat against glass.

The windshield and back window curve horizontally. So your would pull the squeegee across the glass. Since you might not be able to reach the other side of the window, start your strokes from the middle of the wetted window. You will leave a water line in the center, but it can't be helped. Just wipe it with a clean, dry rag.

Side Windows

Most side windows are curved vertically, so, after you wet the window, pull the squeegee down around the curve.

Remember, go with the glass curve not against it.

DIAMOND SHAPED FRENCH WINDOWS

Diamond shaped French windows are just regular French windows except they are angled. The trick is to follow along the moldings. Even though they are angled, just follow the angle.

If you need a smaller squeegee channel, you can cut the one you have with a hack saw or buy a smaller channel. (See appendix.)

HELPFUL HINTS

Removing Calcium Deposits

Those white spots, commonly called calcium deposits or water deposits, are what is left after water dries on the window repeatedly over a period of time.

Usually they are formed by lawn sprinklers hitting the windows or bathroom showers spraying against the doors. It is a common problem in cities with high amounts of minerals in the water supply (hard water).

To fix the problem use Soft Scrub™ or Shower N Stuff™ or products containing oxalic acid. Scrub with a soft WHITE 3M SCOURING PAD to clean off the the deposits. Only the white-colored pad can be used to scrub the window without scratching the glass. (Sometimes they are called polishing pads.) Once you have cleaned off the deposits, apply "Invisible Shield" by Unelco to put a protective coating on the glass. Squeegeeing the window frequently helps keep these deposits from forming also.

CAUTION: Follow all the precautions and warnings placed on the products by the manufacturer.

Removing Artificial Snow Spray

The majority of those snow-in-a-can products can be removed with straight ammonia applied with a sponge.

Ammonia not only removes the fluff but the dreaded residue that usually gets left on the glass. Apply the ammonia with a damp sponge to the artificial snow. Scrub the window till the artificial snow is loosened then wash and squeegee the window. (Warning: be careful not to inhale the ammonia fumes.)

MORE HELPFUL HINTS

1) Sometimes after you have cleaned a window you notice a streak, but you can't tell which side of the window it is on. Some window cleaners avoid this by pulling the squeegee down a window on the outside and across the window on the inside. If the streak appears going down the window you know it's on the outside. If the streak appears going across the window you know the streak is on the inside.

2) With only 2 inches of wet window and 12 inches of squeegee, you know the rubber will squeak on the glass. Avoid rubber squeaking and friction by wetting the rubber with a sponge before you start. The water will lubricate the rubber enough to let it glide smoothly over the glass.

3) Use a spray bottle filled with rubbing alcohol on French windows. Spray four windows, scrub them, and squeegee. The alcohol will evaporate, leaving nothing to wipe.

APPENDIX

If you are serious about becoming the most professional window cleaning company possible, then *I highly recommend* you join the International Window Cleaning Association.

The IWCA was created to give you a place to learn how to become the best window cleaning company. In the IWCA you will find hundreds of highly successful men and women that know what it takes to grow a successful business; they have experienced the growing pains of the beginning, growing and maturing stages of the window cleaning business. *If you have questions. the IWCA has answers.*

International Window Cleaning Association

1-800-875-4922

Or, visit their website at www.iwca.org

ORDER FORM

Order more copies of these books.

How to Clean Windows Like The Pros $9.95

Number of copies ___@ $9.95 $ _____

Straight Talk About Window Cleaning Bidding $ 19.95

Number of copies ____@ $19.95 $ _____

Total _____

Shipping* _____

* Shipping is $3 for one book, $4 for two books.

Order both books and receive a 10% discount

Crystal Press
1750 Orr Avenue, Simi Valley, CA 93065
Phone: 805-527-4369
Fax: 805-527-3949

Or visit our website at www.crystalpress.org